ALL ABOUT DINOSAURS

SPINOSAURUS

by
Mike Clark

KidHaven
PUBLISHING

PHOTO CREDITS

Abbreviations: l-left, r-right, b-bottom, t-top, c-center, m-middle.
Front Cover: Elle Arden Images. Throughout book: rocks – Nonchanon; leaves – ecco. P2–3: bg – lamkaoo99; front – Herschel Hoffmeyer. P4–5: Herschel Hoffmeyer. P6–7: mikeledray. P8–9: kaesunza. P8: l - MarcelClemens; r – guysal. P9: Evgeniy Mahnyov. P10–11: Kotenko Oleksandr. P11: l – Maridav; m – Freer; r – metha1819. P12–13: phadventure. P12: Valentyna Chukhlyebova. P13: Sofia Santos. P14–15: Iri_sha. P14: Catmando. P15: andrea crisante. P16–17: milosk50. P16: l – Valentyna Chukhlyebova; r - Jake Kohlberg. P17: l – Ralf Juergen Kraft; r - Valentyna Chukhlyebova. P18–19: aleksandr hunta. P18: l – Herschel Hoffmeyer; r – Valentyna Chukhlyebova. P19 – Herschel Hoffmeyer. P20–21: andrea crisante. P20: l – Jake Kohlberg; r – Luis Molinero. P21: Ivan Cholakov. P22–23: Rich Carey. P24: Valentyna Chukhlyebova. All photos courtesy of Shutterstock unless specified.

Published in 2018 by
KidHaven Publishing, an Imprint of Greenhaven Publishing, LLC
353 3rd Avenue
Suite 255
New York, NY 10010

Designer: Matt Rumbelow
Editor: Charlie Ogden

Cataloging-in-Publication Data

Names: Clark, Mike.
Title: Spinosaurus / Mike Clark.
Description: New York : KidHaven Publishing, 2018. | Series: All about dinosaurs | Includes index.
Identifiers: ISBN 9781534523579 (pbk.) | 9781534523555 (library bound) | ISBN 9781534524675 (6 pack) | ISBN 9781534523562 (ebook)
Subjects: LCSH: Spinosaurus–Juvenile literature. | Dinosaurs–Juvenile literature.
Classification: LCC QE862.S3 C53 2018 | DDC 567.912–dc23

Printed in the United States of America

CPSIA compliance information: Batch #CW18KL : For further information contact Greenhaven Publishing LLC, New York, New York at 1-844-317-7404.

Please visit our website, www.greenhavenpublishing.com. For a free color catalog of all our high-quality books, call toll free 1-844-317-7404 or fax 1-844-317-7405.

CONTENTS

Words that appear like **this** can be found in the glossary on page 23.

WHAT WERE DINOSAURS?

Dinosaurs were **reptiles** that once lived on Earth. They lived for more than 160 million years before they became **extinct**.

There were many different types of dinosaurs. They lived on land and in water!

WHEN WERE DINOSAURS ALIVE?

Dinosaurs first lived around 230 million years ago during a period of time called the **Mesozoic** Era. The last dinosaurs became extinct around 65 million years ago.

Millions of years ago, all the land on Earth was together in one piece. Then, during the time of the dinosaurs, it slowly broke up into the different **continents** that we know today.

WHEN ALL THE LAND ON EARTH WAS TOGETHER IN ONE PIECE, IT WAS CALLED PANGEA.

PANGEA

HOW DO WE KNOW...?

We know so much about dinosaurs because of scientists called paleontologists who study them. They dig up **fossils** of dinosaurs to find out more about them.

Scientists put together the bones they find to try to make full dinosaur skeletons. From these skeletons, scientists can often figure out the length and weight of a dinosaur. We can also find out information about what it ate from its fossilized food and waste.

SCIENTISTS HAVE EVEN FOUND FOSSILIZED EGGS AND FOOTPRINTS BELONGING TO DINOSAURS.

SPINOSAURUS

Spinosaurus was one of the biggest dinosaurs to ever live on Earth. It is also believed to be the biggest **predator** ever — even bigger than *Tyrannosaurus rex* (tuh-RAA-nuh-sohr-uhs REHKS)!

NAME	*Spinosaurus* (spy-nuh-SOHR-uhs)
LENGTH	46 feet (14 m)
HEIGHT	20 feet (6 m)
WEIGHT	up to 20 tons (18.1 mt)
FOOD	CARNIVORE
WHEN IT LIVED	97 to 112 million years ago
HOW IT MOVED	walked on two legs

Spinosaurus became extinct around 97 million years ago. Paleontologists believe that the place where *Spinosaurus* lived became dry and this slowly killed *Spinosaurus*.

SPINOSAURUS MEANS "SPINE LIZARD."

WHAT DID SPINOSAURUS LOOK LIKE?

Spinosaurus could grow to be more than 46 feet (14 m) long and had a large skull. Its mouth was filled with large, sharp teeth that were used to grab fish and scare away other dinosaurs.

It also had a large back fin called a sail. Paleontologists still do not know exactly what this was for. Some believe it was used to collect the heat from the sun to help keep *Spinosaurus* warm.

WHERE DID SPINOSAURUS LIVE?

Spinosaurus fossils have only been found in North Africa so far. Paleontologists believe *Spinosaurus* liked to live near water because its fossils have been found near beaches and rivers in Africa.

Spinosaurus shared its home with other dinosaurs, such as *Sarcosuchus* (sar-koh-SOO-kuhs). However, *Sarcosuchus* probably would have eaten the same food as *Spinosaurus*, meaning the two dinosaurs probably would not have got along.

WHAT DID *SPINOSAURUS* EAT?

Spinosaurus is believed to have eaten mostly fish. Paleontologists believe this because *Spinosaurus* had a narrow **snout** and cone-shaped teeth, which are perfect for catching fish.

Paleontologists also believe that *Spinosaurus* might have caught flying reptiles, called pterosaurs (TEH-ruh-sohrs), right out of the air. However, they would only do this when there was not enough food in the rivers.

WAS SPINOSAURUS THE BIGGEST MEAT EATER?

Spinosaurus is believed to be the biggest meat eater to ever walk the earth. It was even bigger than *Giganotosaurus* (jig-uh-NO-tuh-sohr-uhs), which grew to be about 43 feet (13 m) long.

GIGANOTOSAURUS

SPINOSAURUS

Spinosaurus was only the largest predator of its time, not the largest dinosaur. That title goes to the *Argentinosaurus* (aar-juhn-tee-nuh-SOHR-uhs), which could grow to be 115 feet (35 m) long!

ARGENTINOSAURUS

A CLOSER LOOK AT SPINOSAURUS

THE FIRST *SPINOSAURUS* FOSSIL WAS FOUND IN EGYPT IN 1912, BUT SADLY IT WAS DESTROYED DURING WORLD WAR II.

HELP SPINOSAURUS CATCH SOME FISH

GIVE OTHERS A CHANCE TO SOLVE THE MAZE. FIND THE WAY OUT USING YOUR FINGER, NOT A PEN.

GLOSSARY

carnivore an animal that eats other animals rather than plants

continent one of the seven great masses of land on Earth

extinct no longer alive

fossil the remains of old plants and animals that lived a long time ago

Mesozoic a period of time when dinosaurs lived from 252.2 million years ago to 66 million years ago

predator an animal that hunts other animals for food

reptile a cold-blooded animal with scales

snout a type of nose and mouth that sticks out in front of an animal's face

INDEX